PROPHETIC MOVEMENTS

Prophetess
Ikia Smith

LET'S RETHINK THAT
Atlanta, GA
www.letsrethinkthat.com

Prophetess Ikia Smith
smith.ika@yahoo.com

Prophetic Movements © 2016

DEDICATION

This work is dedicated to:
my late maternal grandmother, Lula Lee White,
my paternal grandmother (Momma) Mattie Mae Bryant,
and Helena 'Na-Na" Black.

All three of you have greatly influenced my spiritual walk
with God.

ACKNOWLEDGMENTS

A special thanks to:
Apostle Howard J. Smith,
Amar J. Walls,
Gabrielle M. Smith.

You have been there through the ups and downs of writing this book and getting it finished. Thank you all for your undying supernatural support.

TABLE OF CONTENTS

WHAT ARE PROPHETIC MOVEMENTS?

Prophetic movements are the simply word being manifested in your life. It is God speaking to us in a language or manner that we understand. In the Bible, God spoke to His people using examples they understood. If He spoke to a farmer, He spoke using examples related to farming. If He spoke to a fisherman, He spoke in parables that related to fishing, and so forth and so on. As it was with them, so it is with us! God speaks daily to us in the same way – in a language that we can understand, a language related to something in our lives.

Using prophetic movements is God's way of building relationship with us. God really wants an intimate relationship with us to express His love in ways we have never experienced. He wants us to know that what we feel, He feels. What we see, He sees. He lives in us, and His word is manifested through us. Prophetic movements draw closer to Him. Why? Because he loves us. Jeremiah 31:3 reminds us of this love. "Yes, I have loved you with an everlasting love; therefore, with lovingkindness I have drawn you."

Prophetic movements are a navigational tool used by God show us where we are and where He wants take us. They are God's way of calling us to play our assigned part in a wonderful manuscript He wrote before He formed us in our mother's belly. Prophetic movements are like interpretive dances that help the audience see and understand a story more clearly.

Through prophetic movements, God shows us He is always present. In Hebrews 13:5, He promises to never leave us nor forsake us. We have the comfort of knowing that no matter the test or trial, God will be there. However, there are times when we feel forsaken and it seems like God is not present, speaking, or moving on our behalf. During these times, we feel overlooked and neglected when God does not want us to feel this way. He is ever present is because He loves and cares for us. He is concerned about every aspect of our lives, and He has given us prophetic movements so we can see Him at work on our behalf.

Prophetic movements are here, there, and everywhere. However, we need help to see them.

OUR PROPHETIC HELPER

When Jesus ascended to the right hand side of God the Father, he too promised that He would never leave us or forsake us; he would not leave us comfortless. John 14:16-18; 26 states,

(16) And I will pray the Father, and He will give you another Helper, that He may abide with you forever— (17) the Spirit of truth, whom the world cannot receive, because it neither sees Him nor knows Him; but you know Him, for He dwells with you and will be in you. (18) I will not leave you comfortless; I will come to you. (26) But the Helper, the Holy Spirit, whom the Father will send in My name, He will teach you all things, and bring to your remembrance all things that I said to you.

Ten days after his ascension, Jesus sent us the gift of the Holy Spirit. The Holy Spirit is our comforter - counselor, helper, intercessor, advocate, strengthener, stand by). He is also our guide that helps us to recognize prophetic movements. We would not be able to do so without the Him. It is His responsibility to teach us all things and to bring to our remembrance the prophetic promises that God has made. Being conscious (naturally and spiritually) of what is going on around us, helps us take account of what God is saying. When we rely on the guidance of the Holy Spirit, that is when we receive confirmation, revelation, and manifestation. prophetic movements only come to confirm what God is saying, reveal what God is doing, and manifest or show what God has done.

We need the Holy Spirit to lead us to and through prophetic movements. Prophetic Movements come to communicate whatever needs to be said to us. They acknowledge answered prayers or give us instruction to help us the way through any situation. Prophetic movements guide us when we have questions about our spiritual walk. We need the Holy Spirit help us discern these movements that come in many different ways.

PROPHETIC MOVEMENTS

Prophetic Movements are found in anything God sees fit to use to speak to us including the written and spoken word, situations in life, sickness, and numbers.

The Spoken and Written Word

Hebrews 4:12 says that "the word of God is quick, and powerful, and sharper than any two edged swords..." It means that the word is alive, moveable, and powerful. The word changes lives when it is received. It is the most powerful prophetic movement and comes in two forms – written and spoken. The written word, the Bible, is a progressive revelation that confirms, reveals, and manifests God's plan for the universe and man. Studying the Bible allows God to speak to us through the experiences of others. It allows us to see past prophetic movements to build faith as we journey through prophetic movements today. The Bible contains principles – fixed laws that will not fail – and will continue to stand the test of time, showing that Jesus is the "same yesterday and today and forever" (Hebrews 13:8). The written word does not just pertain to God, but it also relates to us as well. For we have the power to write a vision and carry it out just as God commanded the Prophet Habakkuk, "And the Lord answered me saying, write the vision, and make it plain upon tablets, that he may run that readeth it" (Habakkuk 2:2).

God speaks to us through His spoken word. God created the universe and everything in it with the spoken word. The spoken word is so powerful that God decreed, "So shall My word be that goes forth from My mouth, it shall not return to Me void, but it shall accomplish what I please, and it shall prosper in the thing for which I sent it" (Isaiah 55:11). God has given us that same power - to create prophetic movements – and speak things into existence. Just like God decreed that He shall have whatsoever He says, the same is with us, for "death and life are in the power of the tongue, and those who love it will eat its fruit" (Proverbs 18:21). Words, whether written or spoken, cause things to happen - good or evil. We must be careful of what we speak. There is much more power in what we speak than we could ever know!

Whether written or spoken, God's word changes lives when received. It causes us to incline our ears to listen to God and receive direction. It makes us more inclined to say "yes" to God, which causes us to do things typically out of the ordinary for us.

The Cause and Effect of Saying "Yes"

All of this (my conscious life in God) started with a simple "yes" to God. The Holy Spirit told me to title this chapter "Cause and Effect." When we wholeheartedly say yes to God, we give Him all access, free reign in our lives, which *causes* an almost immediate *effect*. We hear preachers say it all the time from the pulpit: "When we say 'yes' to God, we really do not know what we were saying 'yes' to." We have to trust and belief that God loves us more than we can fathom and has our best interests at heart.

The "yes" sometimes comes easily. At other times, the "yes" comes after doing or seeking after other things. When we have done all we can do to accomplish what we believe is the purpose of our existence and we are still unfilled, that is when we throw our hands up and really say "yes" to God. It is a beautiful thing because it shows us without a shadow of doubt that we need God to truly have inner joy and peace – peace that goes beyond our understanding.

My "yes" started when I was 18 years old. I was a single teenage mother living in Memphis, Tennessee. I worked a job during the week, and I did hair from home on the weekends. I was at a point where I needed a change from the drama I was experiencing (especially with my daughter's father). Seeking direction from God, I heard the Holy Spirit tell me to move to California and enroll in cosmetology school. He told me to leave right after Thanksgiving, which meant that I would miss Christmas. I was torn because Christmas was a special time for me and my family, but I obeyed God. I moved to California with my father and enrolled in cosmetology school in 1995. (In retrospect, God knew that if I waited until Christmas, I would not have left and would have continued in drama-filled situation delaying or missing the prophetic move of God.)

While in school in California, the Holy Spirit began to dwell in my life. I found myself alone a lot communing with God. Through God's guidance, I moved out of my father's house into my own place. In 1996, I graduated from cosmetology school, got my license, and began establishing myself in my career. The money was good; however, I was still unfulfilled. As a result, I ended up in the "wrong hands" and had a son in 2000. After the birth of my son, I looked at my life and decided to make major changes. Thank God that by this time I *really* realized I could not make those changes without His guidance. I needed to focus on my children and their future. I did not want to be involved with any man because obviously I was doing something wrong when it came to love and relationships. I pretty much had decided that I would probably be single for the rest of my life. I would devote myself to being the best mother possible to my then newborn son and 8-year old daughter. I was fine with it. Seemingly as soon as I had accepted this status, the Lord dropped a husband into my spirit. At that moment, I looked around and said, "Where did this come from?" I was excited at the thought of getting married, yet in denial at the same time. Immediately, I asked God, "Where is this husband of mine?" No answer....at least not yet.

God told me to make a trip to Memphis for Easter (2001). He said that I was to help find my mother a church home. I obeyed. She told me that she watched this church on TV, so that is where we went to worship. My mother and I enjoyed Easter service so much that we decided to attend Bible Study that week. At Bible Study, I saw this guy who looked very familiar. After service, I approached him and asked him his name and where attended high school. His name was Howard, and it turned out I knew him from high school, but he was not the same "hoodlum" from a few years back. God had changed his whole identity. He gave me a prophetic word, and we exchanged numbers. Shortly thereafter, I went back to California and continued with my plans for my children and I to move into a larger as we had outgrown the one-bedroom apartment in which we were living, but God told me to stand still and wait.

In the midst of my waiting, Howard and I became reacquainted. I would call Howard for spiritual counseling, but he would not stay on the phone with me for no more than three minutes at a time. It was frustrating to me because I knew he had something for me from God. I could sense prophetic movement even in the midst of waiting. However, it would not be revealed until several months later on October 1, 2001.

During an *hour* long phone conversation, God revealed that Howard was my husband and I was his wife. Howard told me that God had told him that he would find his wife in that particular church my mother and I visited together. Gold revealed to both of us that in order to get to the next phase or dimension in Him, we needed each other. From that exchange, the decision was made to get married. There was not an overdramatic proposal – just the prophetic movement of God in the form of divine revelation.

Engaged, my children and I moved back to Memphis. However, Howard and I decided to get married in California. At the bus station on the way to California, we were approached by a cross dresser, who removed of his female attire beforehand. He prophesied to us, referring to my sweat suit and earring wearing husband as "preacher" and telling us things only God could have revealed to him.

During the marital transition, other supernatural things happened. Going to Memphis, my children and I flew. Being that it was right after 9/11, Los Angeles International (L.A.X.) was chaotic. There were lines for miles, soldiers with guns, and every other kind of security imaginable. You had to arrive to check in three hours early. When we arrived at the airport, we got in line outside the terminal. There was only one entrance open for security reasons. As we stood patiently, I noticed locked glass doors to my right. All of a sudden, a man came out of the locked glass doors. He was an older black man in uniform. He came and asked me to follow him. He said he wanted to get me and the children out the traffic and exhaust fumes. I was relieved. We followed him through the glass doors, passing the lines of those who had been waiting and into a double sided elevator. While in the elevator, fear came over me. His back was turned to me. He sensed the fear and immediately said the same thing he said to me when he approached us in line, "Do not be afraid." The doors opened on the other side of the elevator. My children and I exited. I turned around to say "thank you" and he told me to "have a safe trip." I called Howard and told him what happened. He immediately said the stranger was an angel. There was no other explanation! God sent an angel to ensure our well-being. Out of all of the people in line, he walked up to us to escort us to safety. What divine favor! What awesome prophetic movement! However, this was just the beginning...

We found ourselves in Memphis for three months before God commanded me to return to California with the children. It did not make any sense. Why would God have us move across country only to move back *without* my new husband right before Valentine's day and his birthday? I wanted to be with my husband. God asked me, "Do you think *I will not* be in California when you get there?" God wanted to make sure that I knew this move was about His divine purpose and plan and not my husband. As I have heard so many times before, God is a jealous God. As a result, I got my priorities straight and my children and I returned to California. I quickly found a place for us to live and started working. Two months later, Howard arrived in California only to find out (that in our absence God) was calling him to the apostleship.

Over the next few months, my husband worked to establish King's Dominion World Worship Ministries. I became pregnant and gave birth to our daughter in February 2003. In 2004, God moved us from Inglewood to Lancaster, California. Before that move, God told me to turn all the finances over to Howard. I was the only one working. To give up control of the money I was earning was a tough pill to swallow. Nevertheless, I trusted God. After three months in Lancaster, God told Howard that we were to move back to Memphis. It seemed like just as we were getting settled, God would have us move.

We drove from California to Memphis in a Ford Explorer with our children, all of our possessions, and $200. Since our return in February 2005, God has not failed us. As we drove across country, God brought to my remembrance Steve Wonder's song, "Don't You Worry 'Bout a Thing!" The lyrics of the song ministered to me.

Don't you worry 'bout a thing
Don't you worry 'bout a thing, mama
Cause I'll be standing on the side
When you check it out...Yeah

When you get it off...your trip
Don't you worry 'bout a thing...Yeah
Don't you worry 'bout a thing...Yeah

Through this prophetic movement (in song), God reminded me of His promise to never leave or forsake me. God reminded me that (be)*cause* I gave him a wholehearted "yes," the *effect* was He would lead, guide, and show the way. Even though I had negative relationship experiences, through prophetic movements, God led me a husband after His own heart. God reminded that (be)*cause* I gave him a yes, the *effect* was that He would withhold no good thing from me. All (be)*cause* I gave God a yes, the *effect* is I will go where He wants to go, even if that means moving from Tennessee to California back to Tennessee back to California, from Inglewood to Lancaster and then back to Tennessee, and do what He wants me to do. Why? (Be)cause prophetic movements confirm what God is saying, reveal what God is doing, and manifest what God has done.

Sickness

Right before we left Inglewood, California in 2004, I was still struggling with my yes to God. I was fairly new to being aware of God's prophetic movements in my life at that time. One night in that struggle, I had a dream in which my left forearm was missing. I asked myself, "How can I do hair without both hands?" I was perplexed. Five years later, in October 2009, I unexpectedly had brain surgery, which left me with numbness in my left forearm. Three years later, in 2012, God revealed to me that being a stylist was not my only purpose in life, but that I would write – this book in particular. It then I understood the dream from years earlier. God was telling me that regardless if I had one hand or two, I was going to fulfill my life's purpose. My (resulting condition from) brain surgery was not unto death, but for the glory of God, that the Son of God might be glorified thereby (John 11:4). This numbness in my left forearm that I experience to this day is a constant reminder of the divine purpose on my life.

Numbers

Throughout the Bible, numbers are used to confirm, reveal, or manifest the prophetic move of God. Below are examples of the significance of the numbers 1-10 as revealed in the Bible.

1- **Singleness of Purpose/God the Father**

> Genesis 1 reveals that everything started with God – a single entity or spirit.

2- **A Balance of Total Opposites**

> There are two parts of a 24-hour period – night and day. That work in conjunction with the sun and moon. There are two sexes in the human race – male and female (Genesis 1).

3- **The Holy Trinity (God the Father, God the Son, & God the Holy Spirit)**

> Scripture reveals to us, although they are one, there are three distinct personalities that comprise the Godhead - God the Father, God the Son, and God the Holy Spirit (Mathew 28:19).

4- **Balance**

> Four represents balance. For example, the four seasons, our hands and feet (four parts or units, the four corners of a building or a room. The number four symbolizes establishment and authority (Revelations 7:1).

5- Grace

Human beings have five fingers to praise God (2 Corinthians 12:9-10) and five toes to stand in blessing (John 13:1-17). There are fivefold ministry gifts: Apostle, Prophet, Evangelist, Pastor, and Teachers (Ephesians 4:11).

6- Man

Man was created on the sixth day (Genesis 1:27). Six is a double dose of everything (Exodus 20: 9,11).

7- Completion and Perfection

The Lord rested on the seventh day after creating. Like four, seven also means balance. It establishes order (Revelations 4:5); God has seven spirits.

8- New Beginnings

God saved eight people on the ark in order to have a new beginning for mankind after the flood (1 Peter 3:18). In the Hebrew culture, males were circumcised on the eighth day after birth to represent God's covenant with man (Genesis 17:10).

9- Birthing or Fertility

Human births take place after nine months for pregnancy - the completion of a cycle. There are nine fruits of God's Holy Spirit: Faithfulness, Gentleness, Goodness, Joy, Kindness, Long suffering, Love, Peace and Self-control (Galatians 5:22 - 23).

10- Divine Order

God gave Moses Ten Commandments to govern the people of Israel (Exodus 20). A tithe, God's giving requirement, is a tenth (Genesis 14:20; 28:22; Leviticus 27:30; 2 Chronicles 31:5; Malachi 3:10).

God uses numbers to demonstrate prophetic movement. God has used numbers to guide me when making major life decisions. He has also used numbers to indicate a natural and/or spiritual positioning. My birthday and my husband's birthday are on the 17th, which signifies VICTORY. Therefore, our natural and/or spiritual positioning is always one of victory. I have seen prophetic movement in the addresses of several places we have lived. The number 15 means rest in total faith in God. We have lived in three places that add up to the number 15. All that says to me is that God has not left us or forsaken us.

I only provided the significance of the numbers 1-10 as a starting base. However, there are a number of resources (i.e. Strong's Concordance, Eight-day Assembly website) that provide the meaning of Biblical numbers beyond the number 10. I challenge you to example the prophetic movements in your life through numbers to see what God is saying to you.

NAVIGATING PROPHETIC MOVEMENTS

Throughout our lives, we will experience many prophetic movements. What do we do when we encounter a prophetic movement? How do we successfully navigate them? We successfully navigate them with prayer, discernment, and faith.

Prayer

Our prayers should be conversations with God. Prayer helps us to navigate prophetic movement. Sometimes it is good to just incline our ears and listen to God instead of always talking to Him. God hears our prayers – period, and we have to trust that God answers our prayers before we even ask. We have to talk to God as if He is right in front of us, know that He has processed it, and that He will deliver. He is the only one we can go to that can really help us. God is always directing us to His kingdom - His way. Matthew 6:33 says, "But seek first the kingdom of God and His righteousness, and all these things shall be added to you." What things will be added? All things! What is after all? ALL. When we pray, we need to really ask God what does He wants us to do. What is His way? How does He want us to navigate the prophetic movements occurring in our lives?

The only way to know how God wants us to navigate prophetic movements is to listen to His instruction after we have prayed. It is vital to know when God is speaking. One way we can tell when God speaks to you is there is peace in our spirit. James 1:17 states, "Every good gift and every perfect gift is from above, and comes down from the Father of lights, with whom there is no variation or shadow of turning." There will be a peace in our spirit that goes beyond our understanding and we will be able to stand on it.

Discernment

Discernment plays a big part in prophetic movements. Spiritual discernment is calling on the Holy Spirit to lead or give direction on a matter. It is a gift from God. It is governed by love (1 Corinthians 13:1-3). Discernment centers us onto Jesus the Christ and Lord (1 Corinthians 12:3) and His good news. It directs us to scripture, not away from it (Isaiah 8:19-20). It builds up the church and its members (Ephesians 4:11-12) giving it power, wisdom, character, boldness, and unity. It helps create in us a love of righteousness, a heightened sense of sin, and a turning away from known evil.

When discerning prophetic movements, we must keep in mind why we are doing it. We have to yield ourselves to the spirit and pay attention to what He is saying through our actions. It gives us a sense of what God is doing now and what role we play in it. The gift has spiritual eyes for cutting through façades and confusion to get to the heart of the matter. We will know when we have discerned a movement because we will have a sense of peace and clarity about it.

Discernment is knowing when God is speaking on something that has happened, happening, or going to happen. It is a spiritual insight to the physical manifestational flow of the spirit. It can become quite difficult to explain, but as we walk with God, we tune in to what is going on around us more. It is nothing we have to seek or look for; the movements are all around us. All we have to do is pay attention.

I constantly look for physical manifestations of Him – a prophetic move. I had to pull on the Holy Spirit for clear discernment of the movements I noticed happening. The Holy Spirit will give us scripture for any particular movement – all we have to do is ask. Discernment builds the body. In other words, it edifies. In 1 Corinthians 14:26 says, "let all things be done unto edifying." When we come together and sing a psalm, hear a sermon, tongues go forth, a revelation, or interpretation, God uses prophetic movements to edify or build the body.

Love is most important when it comes to discernment. Without it, we accomplish nothing in God. 1 Corinthians 13 says, "you can prophesy, speak with the tongues of men and angels, understand all mysteries, all knowledge, have all faith, feed the poor, give your body to be burned, if there's no love, there's no profit."

An example of God's love shown through discernment is in 1 Samuel 15. Samuel was grieved by Saul being rejected by God as king. God sent to tell Saul to utterly destroy all the spoils of the land including the livestock. Saul chose to spare the spoils of the land and destroy what he felt was useless. Samuel discerned that Saul was lying to him when he inquired about it. He also heard sheep and oxen that should have been destroyed still alive. Samuel turned to worship God alongside Saul whom he knew Saul had disobeyed God. It took love to do that. He could have easily walked away, but he worships God and to love Saul in spite of his disobedience to God.

Faith

When I would hear the word, "faith," I wondered what did it really mean. The Holy Spirit gave me a formula for faith. He revealed to me that faith is obedience, belief, and patience. To navigate prophetic movements, we need all three. Obedience to move, belief to continue to move, and patience to see it through. Until we are strengthened in our faith, obedience is an umbrella for belief and patience.

Obedience. The best way to express our love to God is to obey Him. Saying we love God is one thing, but when we obey Him, we show our love. When God gives us instructions, it is usually something that takes all of our mind and strength to accomplish. Hebrews 4:11 AMP states, "Let us therefore be zealous and exert ourselves and strive diligently to enter into that rest or belief of God, to know and experience it for ourselves, that no one may fall or perish by the same kind of unbelief and disobedience into which those in the wilderness fell." It takes a lot out of us. Although God uses us to accomplish His will, we must be mindful that it is not about us. We were created for the sole purpose to fulfill God's will - not ours. We must obey God and know that God has us covered no matter what.

Belief. The word "belief" is defined as the acceptance that something exists or a statement is true. When we accepted Christ and began this Christian journey, we acknowledged the creative, redemptive, and empowering work of God. However, accepting this fact was just the beginning. As it relates to many things and people in our lives, our minds had to be renewed. We have to believe, especially when tempted to return to old habits, that "therefore if any man be in Christ, he is a new creature: old things are passed away; behold, all things are become new" (2 Corinthians 5:17). In order to wholeheartedly believe God at his word, there has to be a renewing of the mind. The Bible admonishes us, "be not conformed to this world: but be ye transformed by the renewing of your mind, that ye may prove what is that good, and acceptable, and perfect, will of God" (Romans 12:2). Belief and reaffirmation of that belief helps us to continue moving forward in the midst of doubt, despair, discouragement, or anything else that comes to hinder our faith.

Patience. In the Bible, I have read more scriptures that speak to our Christian "walk" as opposed to our Christian "run." When we talk about our Christian walk, we use the section of Hebrews 12:1 that says, "let us run with patience the *race* that is set before us" that actually describes a run. Whether walking or running, the key to successfully completing the race is knowing how to pace ourselves – step by step, moment by moment, mile by mile. At times, we are going to go very fast and at times very slow. The pace does not matter as long as we are moving in the right direction.

Patience is not something we learn. We just have to be. There is a time and season for everything – Gods appointed time, which is why prophetic movements are so important to the body of Christ. They bring reaffirming awareness of God's presence in our lives, especially in slow moving times in our Christian walk or run.

CONCLUSION

Prophetic Movements come in different ways to say whatever needs to be said. Prophetic Movements are so awesome because they give insight into God's plans for us. God wants us to "prosper in all things and be in health, just as your soul prospers" and so much more, but the key is recognizing, understanding, and navigating the various prophetic movements. Remember, prophetic movements guide us when we have questions about our own spiritual walk. Prophetic movements are found in numbers, colors, seasons, sicknesses, people, animals, and anything else God sees fit to speak to us. All we need is the guidance of the Holy Spirt to identify them. They are here, there, and everywhere!

REFLECTION QUESTIONS

Now that you have finished the book, it is time for you to reflect to see how prophetic movements are at work in your life.

Prophetic movements are found in God's written and spoken word, situations in life, sickness, and numbers.

1. What prophetic movements have you experienced (recently) through the written word of God?

_____

_____

_____

_____

_____

_____

_____

_____

_____

_____

_____

_____

_____

2. What prophetic movements have you experienced by God speaking directly to you?

_____

_____

_____

_____

_____

_____

_____

_____

_____

_____

_____

_____

_____

_____

_____

_____

_____

_____

_____

_____

_____

3. When we wholeheartedly say yes to God, we give Him all access, free reign in our lives, which *causes* an almost immediate *effect*.

   How has your life changed since you wholeheartedly said "yes" to God? What prophetic movements have you experienced?

   _____

   _____

   _____

   _____

   _____

   _____

   _____

   _____

   _____

   _____

   _____

   _____

   _____

   _____

   _____

   _____

   _____

   _____

4. Sickness is not always unto death but is often times used to bring glory to God. How has God used sickness in your life for His glory and/or to reveal prophetic movement?

_____

_____

_____

_____

_____

_____

_____

_____

_____

_____

_____

_____

_____

_____

_____

_____

_____

_____

_____

_____

5. God uses numbers to confirm, reveal, or manifest prophetic movement. How has God used numbers in your life? What did those numbers reveal, confirm, or manifest?

_____

_____

_____

_____

_____

_____

_____

_____

_____

_____

_____

_____

_____

_____

_____

_____

_____

_____

_____

_____

6. You can navigate prophetic movements through prayer, discernment, and faith. Which one of these do you rely on most when navigating difficult prophetic movements? Explain. Are there other methods you use?

_____

_____

_____

_____

_____

_____

_____

_____

_____

_____

_____

_____

_____

_____

_____

_____

_____

_____

_____

7. Prophetic movements are found in anything God sees fit to use to speak to us. What are some other things God has used to speak to you that are not mentioned in this book?

_____

_____

_____

_____

_____

_____

_____

_____

_____

_____

_____

_____

_____

_____

_____

_____

_____

_____

_____

_____

_____

Notes

_____

_____

_____

_____

_____

_____

_____

_____

_____

_____

_____

_____

_____

_____

_____

_____

_____

_____

_____

_____

_____

_____

_____

_____

_____

Notes

_____

_____

_____

_____

_____

_____

_____

_____

_____

_____

_____

_____

_____

_____

_____

_____

_____

_____

_____

_____

_____

_____

_____

_____

_____

PROPHETIC MOVEMENTS

Consider the lilies, how they grow: they neither toil nor spin; but I tell you, not even Solomon in all his glory clothed himself like one of these. "But if God so clothes the grass in the field, which is alive today and tomorrow is thrown into the furnace, how much more will He clothe you?   -Matthew 6:28-30.

www.ingramcontent.com/pod-product-compliance
Lightning Source LLC
Chambersburg PA
CBHW061755040426
42447CB00011B/2316